to:

from:

What other being on Earth makes lists of things to do, things to buy, things to strive for?
Only us humans. We are the list makers. Maybe this is one of the qualities that sets us apart
from the rest of God's creatures. Leaving life to chance is easy (. . . and chancy!). Making a list
means you've chosen to take control of your time, your destiny, to fully utilize your God-given
gifts, your talents. You are sending your thoughts toward achievable goals, visualizing a differ-
ent and better world, and showing your intent to do something about it.

I AM BLESSED WITH UNIQUE GOD-GIVEN ABILITIES AND TALENTS. I UTILIZE MY ABILITIES AND
MY INTELLIGENCE TO CREATE A BETTER LIFE, A BETTER WORLD FOR MYSELF, MY FAMILY,
FRIENDS, AND MY COMMUNITY. I ENVISION MYSELF ACHIEVING ALL MY GOALS STARTING HERE
AND NOW. I AM GRATEFUL FOR EVERY GOD-GIVEN OPPORTUNITY TO CREATE SUCCESS IN MY LIFE.

There they are, 1 through 5, in no particular order—on an old envelope, scratch pad, or sheet of notebook paper. It's like the old adage says, "Plan your work and work your plan." Put it on the fridge in plain view, on your desk, or between the pages of your favorite book. Wherever you keep it, look at it often. Then go out and make it happen. But be careful of what you put on your list. By writing it down, you make it "important," and "important" things can begin to live your life for you instead of you living your life.

HERE IS A PEN AND HERE IS A PENCIL,
HERE'S A TYPEWRITER, HERE'S A STENCIL
HERE IS A LIST OF TODAY'S APPOINTMENTS
AND ALL THE FLIES IN ALL THE OINTMENTS

—OGDEN NASH

is my list
of things
to do today

go to the
  bank and
the hardware
store,
  put a new
lock on
  the cellar
door

> ❧ THE TASK AHEAD OF US IS NEVER SO GREAT
> AS THE POWER BEHIND US ❦
>
> —RALPH WALDO EMERSON

It can seem like an endless battle just keeping up with basic maintenance on the little piece of the world we call our own . . .

You're standing there with the trimmer in your hand, staring at that hedge, or maybe the laundry is up to your ears. Your inner voice is whispering, "Why did I wait so long to get to this? This is going to be a miserable, back-breaking job!" You know the job is not going to do itself. So you summon up your strength, your resolve to get it over with, and you start. It's not so bad, you're thinking, as you hum to yourself. Sure, maybe the hedge branches poke and scratch your arms or you just about pass out from the pungent, mildewy aroma of old gym socks, but you're gonna get this done! Determination takes over. You hit your zen stride. Every repetitive motion is like a meditation. You forget about your bills and your kids' grades. You stop worrying about office politics. There is true virtue in the total mindlessness of your task. Although you're grimy and tuckered out, you're smiling. That hedge looks pretty darn good. And those socks—well, now that they're washed and folded, they actually don't smell so bad.

I AM GRATEFUL FOR MY EYES, MY HANDS, AND MY FEET AND THE VITALITY THAT ENABLES ME TO ACCOMPLISH THE SIMPLEST AND THE MOST CHALLENGING TASKS. I AM THANKFUL FOR THE TIME I HAVE TO GET THINGS DONE. I KNOW THAT BY USING THE PHYSICAL ABILITY WITH WHICH I'VE BEEN BLESSED I AM SHOWING MY APPRECIATION TO GOD.

I propose that at the end of the day, when we evaluate today's progress and assess today's accomplishments—if we've done anything at all—we should pat ourselves on the back for what we did do, and forgive ourselves for what we didn't.

forgive ourselves

It's a good feeling to get a chore done, especially if it's something you've been putting off for a while. There's a sense of accomplishment and more than a bit of true relief—which sure beats the nagging guilt of procrastination. When you cross that task off your list, allow yourself to feel good about it. You did it. You took the initiative. An hour ago, you picked up that broom and started sweeping. Now the last corner is dust-free. Cross it off with enthusiasm. Know that you are a better person for facing the task and tackling it. Be satisfied for a minute or two, reward yourself, then attack the next thing on your list.

⊰ THE MAJOR VALUE IN LIFE IS NOT WHAT YOU GET.
THE MAJOR VALUE IN LIFE IS WHAT YOU BECOME ⊱
—JIM RHON

I cross 'em off
as I get 'em
done

but when
this sun
is set

> ⊱ SCIENCE WILL NEVER BE ABLE TO REDUCE THE
> VALUE OF A SUNSET TO ARITHMETIC ⊰
>
> —DR. LOUIS ORR

It's easy to let a miracle slip by without even noticing . . .

Maybe it was a long one, or maybe it just flew by. Maybe you felt some joy, some anger, had a laugh, or even shed a tear or two. Maybe you made some progress (sometimes it's hard to tell). But you've got good reason to congratulate yourself—you're still here, you've survived another day in the life.

And now the western horizon is water-painted in glorious, rich, ever-flowing colors as today goes down in flames. The last embers flicker out as the sun hands the sky over to the moon. No smoke—just a sudden chilly darkness and the twinkle of a few early stars. It was just another day in your life and mine. But look at the send-off it gets! Wow, ain't that somethin'?

I CELEBRATE THE PASSING OF THIS DAY AND THE BIRTH OF THIS NIGHT. I AM GRATEFUL BEYOND MEASURE FOR THE OPPORTUNITIES THAT THIS DAY HAS GIVEN ME TO ACHIEVE, TO GROW, AND TO LOVE, AND TO LIVE. I AM EQUALLY GRATEFUL FOR ALL THE OPPORTUNITIES THIS NIGHT OFFERS ME—TO REFLECT, TO CELEBRATE, TO COMMUNE, TO REST AND REPLENISH MY MIND AND BODY. ALL IS WELL AND RIGHT WITH MY WORLD. THANK YOU, GOD, FOR THIS GLORIOUS DISPLAY AND FOR MAKING ME A SMALL BUT IMPORTANT PART OF YOUR GREAT PLAN.

there's still
more
than a few
things
left

I AM GRATEFUL FOR THE NEXT TASK YET TO BE ACCOMPLISHED, THE NEXT ADVENTURE YET TO BE EXPERIENCED, THE NEXT CHALLENGE YET TO BE OVERCOME. AS I FULLY APPRECIATE THE NOW, I GREET THE NEXT NOW THAT AWAITS ME WITH OPEN ARMS, FILLED WITH VITALITY AND CREATIVITY. AS I AM ABLE TO PAUSE AND FEEL THE JOY OF EACH AND EVERY MOMENT, I AM FEARLESS AND EXCITED ABOUT THE NEXT. I AM PRIVILEGED WITH ALL IN MY LIFE THAT REMAINS TO BE DONE, AND I AM CAPABLE OF ACCOMPLISHING ANY CHALLENGE I CHOOSE TO ACCEPT WITH ENTHUSIASM, POSITIVE ENERGY, AND A GRATEFUL HEART.

No matter how realistic our goals are, how low our expectation level is, how do-able our list of tasks might be, something won't get done. Distractions, changing priorities, procrastination, weather, the limits of time itself—whatever the reason, something will remain incomplete, unaccomplished.

But then, what else are we living for but this very moment and the challenges and adventures that await us? Without things to do, places to go, people to meet, after a while wouldn't life become some kind of sleepwalk? Absent the prayers that are yet to be answered, there would be little reason to draw the next breath.

⊰ I LONG TO ACCOMPLISH A GREAT AND NOBLE TASK,
BUT IT IS MY CHIEF DUTY TO ACCOMPLISH
SMALL TASKS AS IF THEY WERE GREAT AND NOBLE ⊱
—HELEN KELLER

I haven't got to yet

Amazing how a few steps can often make a world of difference in the view . . .

As I walked along the trail from the house to the barn, the sound of autumn leaves crunching under my shoes was a pleasant reminder of times gone by. This was the first time I'd taken the walk since my father passed away—a short trek that he and I had traveled together countless times, one where we discussed everything from the problems of the world to the principles of how a bird flies in the sky. As of late, I hadn't felt much like getting out and about, so this was real progress for me. The farther I walked, the lighter my footsteps seemed, the more rejuvenated I felt. Suddenly, it hit me: the actual process of putting one foot in front of the other was exactly what the doctor ordered. Moving forward, going on with my life was what my dad would have wanted me to do. All it took was taking a walk to remind me of that. One step at a time, I began to feel more of the sun's warmth and sense more of the earth's beauty until, for a moment, I even felt my father beside me. I was taking strides in the healing process, and it all began with a little walk.

⊰ THE GREATEST THING IN THE WORLD IS
NOT SO MUCH WHERE WE ARE, BUT
IN WHICH DIRECTION WE ARE MOVING ⊱

—OLIVER WENDELL HOLMES

go for a walk

say a little prayer

The power of prayer is real and truly amazing. . . . We all scooted our chairs to the table at Grandma's house for Sunday dinner. Grandma turned to the four grandchildren and asked that they say the blessing. We joined hands and the children's voices began in unison . . ." God is great, God is good, let us thank Him for this food. By His hands we are fed. Give us, Lord, our daily bread. Amen." I smiled and remembered my youth and the little prayers I learned from my parents. Every night my brother and I would kneel beside our bunk beds with our eyes shut tight and pray, certain that God heard our every word. "Now I lay me down to sleep, I pray the Lord my soul to keep. If I should die before I wake, I pray the Lord my soul to take. Amen." Quite often we would add ". . . bless Aunt Martha and Uncle Howard" or someone we knew or heard about who needed God's help.

As I have grown older, I have come to realize the true benefits of little prayers—those that resemble the ones I learned as a child. Many days, when I first open my eyes in the morning, I say, "Thank you, Lord, for this beautiful day. Let me make the most of it."

And how many times have all of us barely avoided mishap and/or injury and, without thinking, simply blurted out the words, "Thank God!"? And rightfully so . . . we should thank God often for the blessings that we have and for the angels that guide and protect us. So when you wake tomorrow, when you lie down tonight, when you hear a song you love on the radio, whenever you feel inspired, don't forget to look to the sky and say a little prayer.

GOD, THROUGH PRAYER I GIVE THANKS, ASK FOR FORGIVENESS, GUIDANCE, AND HEALING, AND DRAW CLOSER TO YOU. I BELIEVE STRONGLY AND DEEPLY IN THE IMMEASURABLE POWER AND BENEFIT OF PRAYER. GUIDED BY YOUR LOVING SPIRIT, I KEEP A PRAYER OF GRATITUDE IN MY HEART AND ON MY LIPS AT ALL TIMES. AND I KNOW THAT PRAYER DOES NOT EQUIP ME FOR GREATER WORKS—PRAYER IS THE GREATER WORK. THANK YOU, GOD, FOR THIS POWERFUL AND AWESOME TOOL.

take a
deep breath
of mountain air

Comes a time when the only place you can be is in the moment . . .

It's so quiet. The thin, crisp air seems to sparkle in the bright, transparent sunlight. Kaaa-runch. My boot sinks through the crust of ice that covers last night's newly fallen snow. The world is a crystal cathedral, pristine and perfect. Every tree is a unique sculpture with layers of white on green, with blown-glass icicles glistening from the drooping branches.

I take a deep, refrigerated breath—it stings a little as it cleans out every corner of my lungs. A natural smile blooms across my face. I exhale a small cloud of steam that immediately becomes one with the frigid atmosphere. Has there ever been anything as beautiful as this?

> ⊰ YOU ARE, AT THIS MOMENT, STANDING IN THE MIDDLE
> OF YOUR OWN ACRES OF DIAMONDS ⊱
> —EARL NIGHTINGALE

> ⊰ HOW OLD WOULD YOU BE IF
> YOU DIDN'T KNOW HOW OLD YOU ARE ⊱
> —SATCHEL PAIGE

We are all as great as we can imagine ourselves to be . . .

Like most kids in the neighborhood, I grew up with the dream of one day becoming a big league baseball player. One afternoon I was Johnny Bench behind the plate for the Reds, and the next day I'd show up for the neighborhood game with a #7 on my V-necked T-shirt and the swagger of Mickey Mantle. After many of those games, I would return home and beg my father to come out in the backyard and play some catch—I just could not get enough of baseball. During this phase of my life, and as I grew older and played organized baseball, I took the field and played the game with determination and hustle. I loved the feeling of slipping on my oiled-up glove, pounding it a couple of times with my fist, and getting in position to play the bunt, a screamer down the line, or anything hit my way.

LORD, ALLOW ME TO SAVOR THE MAGIC OF THE MOMENT THAT COMES FROM DOING THE SIMPLE THINGS IN MY LIFE. THESE MOMENTS FILL MY HEART WITH JOY; AND YOU HAVE SHOWN ME THAT A MERRY HEART DOES GOOD. I KNOW THAT MY TIME ON EARTH IS SHORT, AND I CHOOSE TO LIVE THIS BRIEF TIME TO IT'S FULLEST—DOING THAT WHICH SATISFIES MY SOUL AND GLORIFIES YOU. LET ME FIND TIME FOR THE ACTIVITIES THAT MAKE ME SMILE TODAY AND EVERY DAY.

put on
    my glove

    and play some
        catch

it's time
that
I make time
for that

A couple of years ago, on a Sunday afternoon, I found myself putting in some overtime at home on a project for work. I went to the garage to retrieve a box of printer paper from the top shelf. As I pulled the box down, an assortment of items came tumbling down with it. There at my feet was my trusty old infielder's glove. Then it hit me—I had let something that I truly enjoy fall by the wayside. Completely immersed in the daily grind of life, I had not taken time for a simple, uncomplicated treasure. I called my brother and said, "I need your help with something. Come over to the house."

Walking into the backyard, I slipped the glove on, pounded its pocket, and relived those days gone by. I let my imagination run, and for a moment I could hear, "Hey, batter, batter." I threw the ball as high as I could, settled under it, and made a smooth one-handed basket catch, reminiscent of a much younger me. Although the old arm is not what it used to be, that moment reminded me that my imagination is still strong. An hour later, my brother and I were playing catch and grinning from ear to ear. And I was Johnny Bench all over again.

johnny bench all over again

wade the shore
and cast a line

better than a day at work

CREATOR, AT THIS MOMENT I EXPERIENCE COMPLETE APPRECIATION OF THE AWESOME WONDER OF YOUR MASTERFUL HANDIWORK. I FEEL A DEEP AND POWERFUL CONNECTION TO THE EVER-FLOWING ENERGY OF LIFE. THE RIPPLING WATERS OF STREAMS AND RIVERS, THE CHANGING TIDES OF LAKES AND OCEANS ARE A WONDROUS REMINDER OF THIS. AND IT GIVES ME A FEELING OF PEACE, BEING HERE NOW, A PART OF THIS GREAT SCENE.

THERE IS ONLY ONE SUCCESS—
TO SPEND YOUR LIFE IN YOUR OWN WAY
—CHRISTOPHER MORLEY

one that got away

RECIPE FOR A PERFECT DAY

1. "Good to be alive!" disposition

2. Preferably a warm, fall day

3. Rod and reel

4. Southern wind (according to angling legend)

5. Crickets, buckeye shad, or night crawlers

6. Tackle box

7. Wading boots

8. Stringer

9. Body of water (this is the real obvious one)

10. Cap that says "Any day fishing is better than a day at work"

Follow these directions: leave your worries, wade the shore, find the place that "feels" like the perfect spot, stop, inhale, bait hook, sweep rod to your backhand, flick your lure gently into water with smooth follow-through, relax, smile, think up a perfect "big-one-that-got-away" story.

Losing touch doesn't have to mean losing a friend . . .

Here I am, holding a scrap of paper with a phone number. My heart quickens. I pick up the phone and dial.

We were so close those long years ago. We went through it all together—forts and sports, puberty and first crushes, conquests and heartaches. How could we have drifted so far apart that I didn't even have a current number and address until this scrap of paper found its way into my life through a series of chance encounters?

The answering machine picks up the line. I start to hang up, but then I decide to leave a message. What do I say?

"Hey, it's me. Um—I'll explain when you call back. My number is . . . "

A familiar voice comes on the line and excitedly interrupts.

"Is that really you? Oh, my God, I've been thinking about you so much lately!"

We fall right back into our old rhythm. There's nothing awkward at all, and there's so much to say. True friendship endures distance, time, and even neglect.

⊰ THE ONLY WAY TO HAVE A FRIEND IS TO BE ONE ⊱
—RALPH WALDO EMERSON

look up a
long lost
friend
   of mine

sit on
the porch

> ❧ THE SOUND OF A KISS IS NOT SO LOUD AS
> THAT OF A CANNON, BUT ITS ECHO
> LASTS A GREAT DEAL LONGER ❧
>
> —OLIVER WENDELL HOLMES, SR.

Few things we could ever say or do have more meaning than a well-timed kiss . . .

The two wooden rocking chairs sit there on our front porch pretty much unnoticed as the sometimes chaotic routine of work, kids, and the responsibilities of day-to-day living occupy our thoughts and our time. As a matter of fact, it's been months since I've sat for a spell in those wooden chairs.

As I pull up the drive on this particular October day, the southern wind is unusually brisk. I walk up the porch steps, and I notice those chairs, rocking ever so slightly, pushed by the breeze—back and forth, back and forth. It's almost as if the creaking sound is faintly calling out to me. I stop and stare for a moment. Then a familiar voice brings me back to the here and now.

to the here and now

"Hey, Honey . . . " It's the love of my life. I walk across the porch, open the screen door, put my arm around her and guide her to those old chairs. We sit rocking side by side, hand in hand. The wind blows long strands of her hair across her face as it reflects the setting sun. Our eyes meet, we both smile. And then our lips are drawn together for a sweet, simple, perfect kiss.

I KNOW THAT I AM TRULY BLESSED WITH LOVE IN MY LIFE. I KNOW THAT MY ACTIONS SPEAK MUCH LOUDER THAN MY WORDS. THANK YOU, GOD, FOR THIS PRECIOUS MOMENT, THIS OPPORTUNITY TO SHOW A WONDERFUL PERSON, SOMEONE WHO IS SO IMPORTANT TO ME, HOW I FEEL ABOUT THEM—WITH A SMILE, A HUG, OR A KISS. TO HAVE THIS CHANCE IS A TREASURE. TO USE IT IS AN ACCOMPLISHMENT.

and give
my girl
a kiss

start livin',
that's
the next
thing
on my
list

THE IMPORTANT
THING IS THIS:
TO BE ABLE
AT ANY MOMENT
TO SACRIFICE
WHO WE ARE
FOR WHAT WE
COULD BECOME
—CHARLES DU BOS

MY LIFE STARTS AGAIN NOW WITH THESE POWERFUL THOUGHTS, THESE CHOICES: I CHOOSE TO BE HERE NOW, TO LIVE FULLY IN THIS GLORIOUS, GOD-GIVEN MOMENT. I CHOOSE TO REMOVE ALL NEGATIVE THOUGHTS AND EMOTIONS, CLUTTER AND CONFUSION FROM MY CONSCIOUSNESS. I CHOOSE TO EXPERIENCE MY LIFE NOW WITHOUT JUDGMENT, KNOWING THAT ALL IS RIGHT AND GOOD, AND THAT EACH STEP I TAKE ALONG THIS PATH LEADS ME TO GOD'S PERFECT LOVE AND LIGHT.

How does life begin? It begins with a thought. Well, actually, in a perfect world, it begins with two thoughts. Two people, a man and a woman, have a common desire to unite—to express their love for each other and to blend their thoughts and passions to create a new being. These thoughts and desires are human life's beginning. So, life is created, and a baby is born. The baby comes to this new existence with a clean slate—no attitude, no judgment. Day by day, a child quickly learns life lessons, has successes and failures, experiences joy and pain. And somehow, an agenda begins to form. This innocent babe gradually grows into a complex person full of attitudes and judgments—with things to do, with appointments and deadlines, goals to achieve, and money to make. There's no time anymore for experiencing. The slate is too cluttered and the mind too noisy.

But it's never too late to start over, wipe the slate clean, throw out the clutter. How does life begin again? It begins with a thought. "Start living." There's a thought for ya . . .

☆ THE KEY IS NOT HOW TO LIVE BUT WHY YOU ARE LIVING ☆
—CHARLIE "TREMENDOUS" JONES

The true accomplishments in life are moments of simple joy . . .

It's about two hours till another Sunday sundown. There's just enough gas in the can to give this lawn a needed trim. The spring rain has inspired the green shag to reach for the sun, and the dandelions are mocking me as they wave defiantly in the early June breeze. Imagine what this place would look like if I let it slide till next weekend. Mike, next door, has got his yard perfectly manicured as usual, which makes mine look even worse. I've gotta get this done.

But there's that dog. I can't help but laugh. My Lord, he looks dejected. I told him we'd go play Frisbee-fetch at the park about four hours ago, and he keeps looking at me with those

GOD, YOU HAVE GIVEN ME TIME ENOUGH FOR EVERYTHING IMPORTANT. WHAT IS IMPORTANT TO ME IS ALWAYS MY DECISION. I CHOOSE NOW TO DO WHAT FILLS MY LIFE WITH MEANING, WHAT FILLS MY HEART WITH JOY AND FULFILLMENT. WHAT TRULY MATTERS IS EXPERIENCING AND SHARING THE JOY OF LIFE IN THE TIME YOU HAVE GIVEN ME. ANYTHING THAT DOESN'T ENRICH MY LIFE EXPERIENCE CANNOT BE SO IMPORTANT.

it wouldn't change
the course of fate

if cuttin' the grass
just had to wait

watery brown eyes like his heart is breaking into tinier pieces minute by minute. He lets out a sound that starts as a whimper and ends up a moan. Hey, you know what—I could set the alarm two hours early tomorrow and get this grass cut. But, really, would it be the end of the world if I actually waited till next Sunday? It certainly wouldn't matter to the dog. So I grab my keys, the Frisbee, and the leash.

"Come on, boy—get in the truck." He hurls himself into the cab, wagging every extremity with canine delight.

Now he's sprinting across the rolling park grass and leaping for that spinning toy flying saucer. I swear he's grinning as he returns with the slobbery plastic plate of pleasure. I praise him, "Good dog, . . . " grab the disc, and throw a high, sloping, boomerang toss. He takes after it like Seabiscuit running the Kentucky Derby. And I'm thinking, now I've got two things to brag about—the happiest dog in the neighborhood and the longest grass.

As significant as helping a child grow up is giving a child a chance to be a child . . .

"Be a monster, Daddy!" Emily would squeal. She was four or five, and it was one of hundreds of weekend hours we spent at the park. I'd roll my eyes up into my head, slack my jaw, and become a hulking Frankenstein zombie. She'd scream and run in mock-terror through the playground. I'd pretend to be too slow and clumsy to catch her. Other kids would join in the game, taunting and evading the "monster." Emily seemed proud it was her hideous dad who was the object of so much pretend fear and loathing.

But it was the swing that she never tired of, and the thing that totally wore me out. I'd hoist her up over my head on the swing for a few seconds of anticipation, then drop her, tickle-bellied, into a steep pendulum's arc. I would pretend to be so uncoordinated in my pushing attempts that I'd miss Emily's swing altogether and almost fall down. Then, suddenly, I'd grab her feet and pull her up into another steep fall. My clowning caused gales of giggles. A child's uninhibited laughter is truly one of life's most delightful sounds. Emily is all grown up and on her own now. I hope she remembers those cherished hours. I'm certain I'll never forget.

LIFE IS A SPLENDID TORCH WHICH I HAVE A HOLD OF FOR THE MOMENT, AND I WANT TO MAKE IT BURN AS BRIGHTLY AS POSSIBLE BEFORE HANDING IT ON TO FUTURE GENERATIONS

—GEORGE BERNARD SHAW

cause I've got more important things

like pushin' my kid on a backyard swing

I won't
break
my back
for a
million
bucks

I can't
take to
my grave

We actually own nothing in this lifetime. Money, cars, houses, jewelry, our bodies, and even our time—all of these are only borrowed. How can we believe that we own anything when we know that one moment can change life forever?

Abundance is a good and wonderful thing—a truly great reward for vision, belief, and diligent work. But riches alone can't buy a ticket to heaven or one more moment of joy when our Creator calls us home.

Love and Truth are all we own for eternity. Love is the substance of what we are, the very essence of our immortal souls and so lives forever. Truth is what we discover through the infinite wisdom and intelligence of God, and so lives on and on. Love is what we continue to give and receive long after the angel of death takes us from our earthly attachments. Truth is always to be guarded closely, as it is a fragile jewel indeed, and a priceless one.

a priceless one

GOD, AT THIS MOMENT I AM BLESSED WITH GOOD HEALTH, YOUR INFINITE LOVE, AND THE JOY OF KNOWING I HAVE BOTH. MY LIFE IS FILLED WITH ABUNDANCE AND PROSPERITY. HELP ME TO TREASURE EACH AND EVERY EXPERIENCE KNOWING THAT IT REFLECTS YOUR PERFECT LOVE AND LIGHT. THE LOVE I SHARE WITH MY FAMILY AND FRIENDS MAKES ME WEALTHY BEYOND ALL MEASURE AND EACH DAY A RICH ONE. THANK YOU FOR THE ABUNDANCE OF MY LIFE.

why put off till tomorrow what I could get done today

> ⅔ FOR ALL SAD WORDS OF TONGUE AND PEN,
> THE SADDEST ARE THESE, IT MIGHT HAVE BEEN ⅔
>
> —JOHN GREENLEAF WHITTIER

Would now be the right moment if you knew this moment was all you had?

How many times have I said, "When I have the money, . . . " "When I have the time, . . . " "When everything is perfect . . . ?" Here we are, just waiting for that magical someday when real life begins, when all systems are "go." Well, I' got news for ya—this ain't rehearsal, folks! The curtain's up, and, for many of us, intermission's over.

Recognize and honor your passions in life. Pursue them now with all your heart. Every one of us was born blessed with divine purpose and inspiration. Yet we spend most of our lives asking for permission to get started. No one can give us permission but ourselves, and life isn't going to begin someday when we're all rich and famous. It's well under way already and galloping by like a herd o' wild horses. Here's the choice—you can choose a horse, jump on and ride, or you can sit here in the dust complainin' about it.

I AM NOW READY TO LIVE MY LIFE TO ITS FULLEST. I LISTEN TO MY HEART AND FOLLOW THE DEEPEST AND MOST DIVINE DREAMS AND INSPIRATIONS, THE ONES GIVEN TO ME THROUGH THE INFINITE GENEROSITY AND INTELLIGENCE OF GOD. THIS IS WHO I AM—COMPLETELY AND TOTALLY VITAL AND IN AWE OF THIS EXPERIENCE CALLED LIFE—AND I REJOICE IN THE OPPORTUNITIES THAT EVERY DAY BRINGS.

DO NOT TAKE LIFE TOO SERIOUSLY. YOU WILL NEVER GET OUT OF IT ALIVE

—ELBERT HUBBARD

Some say if you're not living on the edge, you can't see the view. Now, we're not advocating risking your life or anybody else's—the middle path is usually the right route to travel. But, you're never gonna know exactly how wide the road is until you slip onto the shoulder a couple of times going 10 MPH over the limit. That'll get your heart pumping a little bit! Whooee! And isn't that how we learn? Touch a flame, you get burned. Put your finger in an electrical socket, you get a new perm. Yeah, most of us have done some stupid things, and it's a miracle we survived. But sometimes, just sometimes, maybe you've just gotta kick up your heels, blow off some steam, raise the roof, cut loose, get crazy, walk on the wild side, celebrate—don't hold back!

And after you've been to the edge and seen the view, you might just decide that your normal, everyday, hum-drum routine is pretty darn great after all . . . or you just might discover a brand new, more adventurous you.

 GOD, I KNOW THERE ARE TIMES WHEN I NEED TO RELEASE THE PENT-UP TENSIONS THAT COME FROM EVERYDAY LIVING. I ASK FOR YOUR BLESSING AND YOUR GUIDANCE IN FINDING HEALTHY AND CONSTRUCTIVE WAYS TO LET GO OF STRESS AND ANXIETY. I ASK FOR YOUR FORGIVENESS AND FOR YOUR PERMISSION TO FORGIVE MYSELF IF EVER AND WHENEVER I CROSS THE LINE IN MY EXUBERANCE. I AM FILLED WITH VITALITY. HELP ME TO USE IT WELL.

raise a little hell

laugh till it hurts

Everybody's experienced the doubled-over, can't-catch-your-breath, rolling-on-the-ground kind of laughter. Funny how we never think about it while we are in the moment, but being in that blissful yet somewhat painful state sets us free from any preoccupations we might have. What a wonderful blessing! There is a profound reason people love to tell and hear jokes—to hear others laugh and to laugh themselves—it's part of our very nature. How many times have you been walking down a flat-as-a-board hallway with absolutely no obstacles and tripped? And undoubtedly, you always look back to see what strange and unexpected object was lying there, only to find what you already knew: Either the mysterious obstacle was invisible, or nothing was there at all!! So we simply walk on, shaking our heads and chuckling under our breath—at ourselves.

When couples who have been married for many years are asked what keeps them together, they always have the same response—a sense of humor. Let's laugh at ourselves, laugh at a joke, laugh at life, laugh till it hurts. Laughter heals—it is a divine gift from God. And, after all, it is the best medicine.

⊰ THE MOST WASTED OF ALL DAYS IS
ONE WITHOUT LAUGHTER. ⊱
—E. E. CUMMINGS

Our very humanity is defined by our every act of generosity . . .

At the end of the month we routinely pull out our checkbook and pay our bills. We are charged for electricity and/or gas, water, telephone, and so on. All of these services are provided for us on a conditional basis—we only get what we pay for. If we don't pay the phone bill, the phone company disconnects the line. Forget to pay the electric bill, and you could find yourself in the dark. The only thing that is provided for us unconditionally is God's Love. Yet when it comes time to give to our church, our spiritual family, come on, admit it, most of us give less than we are really able to afford.

As my minister once put it, "What if God billed?" What if the meter was always running on God's bounty? What if all of the wonderful gifts in our lives were given to us at a charge? How much would a clear, crisp, fall day be worth? How about a drenching rain in the middle of a drought that saves the farmers' crops? God's gifts are worth much more than monetary value could represent. For all that we receive shouldn't we give back, and then some?

 I KNOW GOD'S LOVE IS UNCONDITIONAL AND DOESN'T REQUIRE PAYMENT. I DEEPLY APPRECIATE MY SPIRITUAL FAMILY BECAUSE THEY ARE ALWAYS THERE FOR ME AND FOR EACH OTHER. I PRAY FOR A GENEROUS HEART AND THE ABILITY TO SUPPORT THE MESSAGE AND THE MISSION OF MY CHURCH. I KNOW THAT BY GIVING TO MY CHURCH I AM GIVING TO MYSELF. I GRATEFULLY CHOOSE TO SHARE THE BOUNTY OF MY BLESSED LIFE WITH MY CHURCH COMMUNITY.

FROM WHAT WE GET
WE MAKE A LIVING,
WHAT WE GIVE HOWEVER
MAKES A LIFE

—ARTHUR ASHE

put an
extra five
in the plate
at church

call up
    my folks
    just to chat

Sometimes, for no real reason at all is the very best reason to keep in touch . . .

"Hi, Mom."

"Is that you, Son? Is everything all right? You're not sick or in trouble are you?"

"Yeah, it's me, Mom. No, I'm fine, just fine. Really. Is Dad there?"

"Do you have some news?"

"Not really—just put Dad on the other line, would you, Mom?"

"Okay . . . hold on just a minute."

"Hmmm, hello . . . Buddy?"

"Yeah, Dad, hi. Are you both on the phone?"

"What are you up to, Son?"

"Nothing, I really called just to say hi, and . . . "

"What? . . . and what?"

"Well, just to say—I just called to tell you that . . . I love you, that's all."

"Okay . . . well, we knew that."

"I know, Dad—I just kinda wanted to say it. How've you been? . . . "

I AM ETERNALLY GRATEFUL TO MY PARENTS FOR ALL THEY'VE GIVEN ME. I SAVOR THE OPPORTUNITIES TO EXPRESS MY AFFECTION AND GRATITUDE TO THEM FOR THEIR SACRIFICES AND FOR TEACHING ME, THROUGH THEIR WORDS AND DEEDS, WAYS TO LIVE AND WAYS NOT TO LIVE. I AM AT PEACE WITH THE KNOWLEDGE THAT THEY'VE ALWAYS DONE THE BEST THEY COULD DO UNDER ANY AND EVERY CIRCUMSTANCE. MY LOVE FOR THEM IS UNCONDITIONAL, AND SO I ALWAYS LET THEM KNOW.

THE TIME IS ALWAYS RIGHT TO DO WHAT IS RIGHT
—DR. MARTIN LUTHER KING, JR.

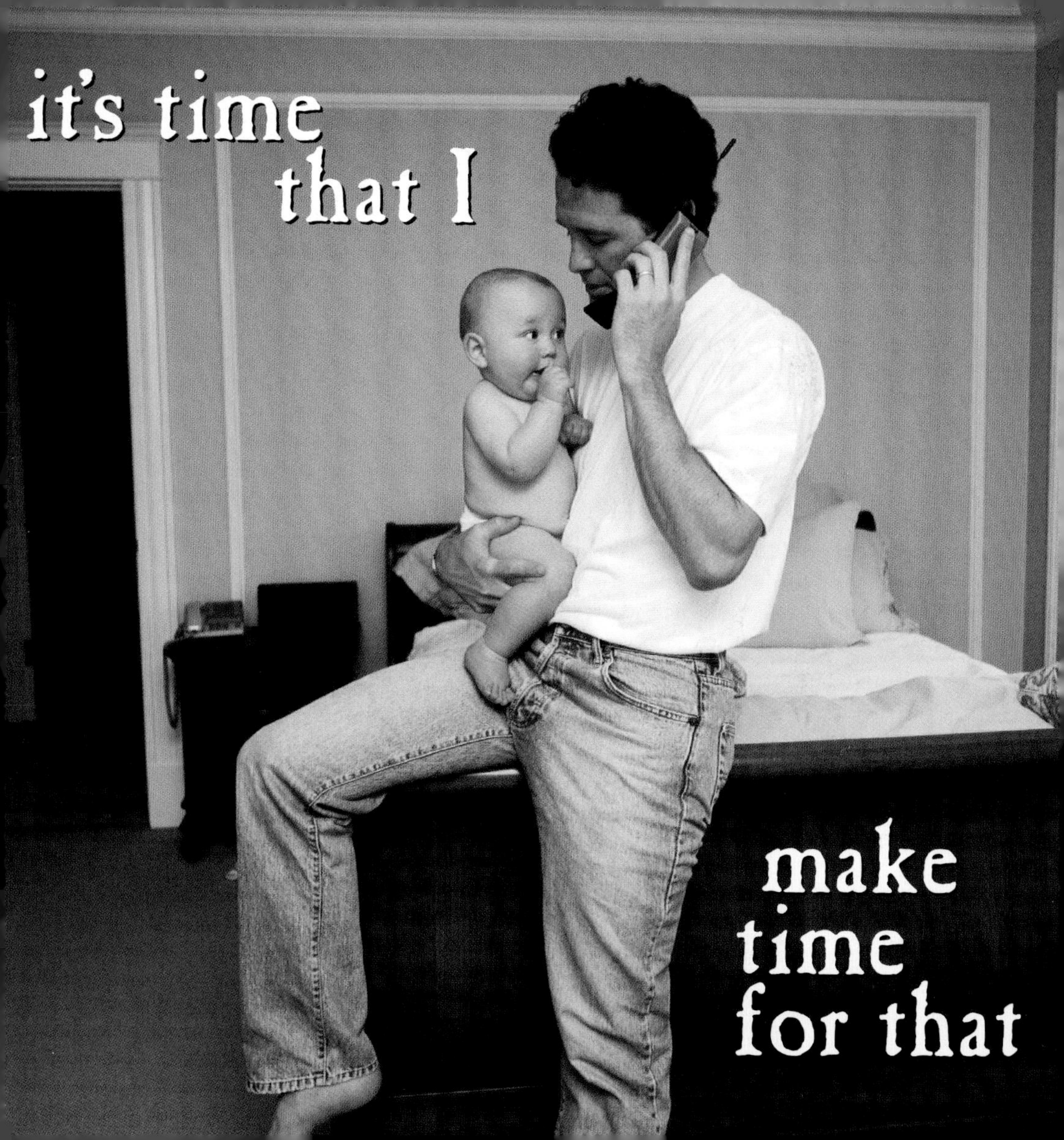

it's time
that I

make
time
for that

There may be the rare occasion that early to bed and early to rise is not the perfect plan . . .

The dinner was incredible—Stacey's linguini and clams. Our daughters, who are like sisters, Glendyn and Elizabeth, have parked themselves in front of a video with hot fudge sundaes. The four adults get busy bussing the table, and in no time the dishes are done. We've caught up on all the personal news.

As we relocate to the living room, our exchange continues through books, movies, politics, and stories about angels and miracles. The energy flows without effort. Each of us shines and shows moments of his or her true brilliance. We laugh. We are all amazed, enthralled, captivated by the stimulating dialogue. "These are great friends," I'm thinking.

Then I glance at the clock. I can't believe it—it's 1:30 A.M.! Nobody even noticed the time slipping away. As our friends trundle to their car in the deep dark of a flawless Friday night, I take my wife in my arms and make a suggestion.

"Let's sleep in."

"Good idea," she whispers in response. I put my arm around her, and we walk to the bedroom.

DEAR GOD, I AM GRATEFUL TO BE LIVING IN THIS MIRACULOUS TIME FULL OF TREMENDOUS CHANGE AND OPPORTUNITY. I CELEBRATE EACH AND EVERY DAY WITH AN OPEN HEART. I SAVOR EACH MOMENT OF MY LIFE FULLY, KNOWING THAT EVERY MINUTE IS UNIQUE AND IRREPLACEABLE AND OFFERS YET ANOTHER CHANCE TO GROW EVER CLOSER TO YOU AND TO KNOW YOUR PERFECT LOVE. THANK YOU, THANK YOU, THANK YOU FOR MAKING ME A PART OF YOUR UNIVERSAL PLAN OF LOVE AND LIFE.

stay up late
and oversleep

‡ LIFE IS A GREAT BIG CANVAS,
AND YOU SHOULD THROW ALL
THE PAINT YOU CAN ON IT ‡

—DANNY KAYE

show her what
she means to me

⊰ AND WHEN LOVE SPEAKS, THE VOICE OF ALL THE GODS
MAKES HEAVEN DROWSY WITH THE HARMONY . . . ⊱
—WILLIAM SHAKESPEARE

A few simple words or the smallest gesture can reveal our deepest feelings . . .

She taught me everything I know about being a human being. Oh, yeah, it's hard to understand the way she thinks or the things she does sometimes. But her smile, her touch, the way she lets me be the ornery fool I'm prone to be and still keeps me around. . . . My Lord, how could I not be grateful for her grace, her generous spirit? Wouldn't I be an even bigger fool if I didn't say or do something now and then to let her know how much I appreciate her? Flowers always work. A card—women love cards. But, wait a minute—what if I get hit by a bus on the way to the florist, or the earth opens up and I fall into a deep, dark crevice before I get to the card shop? She wouldn't have a clue that I'm thinking about what she means to me right now. I guess I'll just have to come right out and tell her.

"I love you, Darlin."

"You do?"

"Yeah, I do . . . I mean it."

"That's good. I'm glad . . . I love you, too."

catch up on all the things

I've always missed

IT'S NEVER TOO LATE TO BE
WHAT YOU MIGHT HAVE BEEN
—GEORGE ELIOT

All is possible with vision, passion, and, ultimately, action . . .

It's like unwrapping a dusty present that's been sitting on the closet shelf for years. It's about asking your heart of hearts these questions—"What do I really love to do? What truly nurtures me?" You might be surprised at your own answers.

What is it you've been denying yourself because the timing's never right? What have you never given yourself permission to truly explore because it's just too crazy to consider? What is the thing that makes your heart beat faster when you start daydreaming about it? Think big! Is it going back to school to get that degree? Maybe adopting an orphan who would thrive with your love and care. Have you been longing to dedicate yourself to a cause or a campaign you care deeply about?

> I BELIEVE THAT LIFE IS FULL OF JOY AND LOVE AND BEAUTY. I KNOW THAT I WAS CREATED TO
> EXPERIENCE ALL THAT IS GOOD IN LIFE—ABUNDANCE, SUCCESS, POSITIVE RECOGNITION,
> GOOD HEALTH, HAPPINESS, AND FULFILLMENT. I CHOOSE TO THINK THE THOUGHTS AND DO
> THE THINGS THAT GIVE MY LIFE THESE QUALITIES AND TO SURROUND MYSELF WITH THOSE
> THAT RECOGNIZE AND APPRECIATE THESE QUALITIES IN ME AND IN MY LIFE. THANK YOU,
> GOD, FOR GIVING ME THIS CHANCE TO LIVE THIS WONDERFUL LIFE.

Get excited! Feel the rush! Lose some sleep. Wake up grinning ear to ear, in love with life and possibility again. Whatever it is, don't wait. Put your life where your heart is. Start the ball rolling now! Go ahead and sign up for the Peace Corps. Sit down and write that novel. When you put your head on your pillow every night, do it knowing that you did something today that you truly love. Put something on your list for yourself. Put your dream in motion and feel good about it. You deserve it.

God created us with passions, vision, and talent—if what we're doing now isn't joyful, then we've ignored or pushed aside the true reason we were created. Don't insult your Creator by disregarding your real reason for being. Do the heart stuff . . .

do the heart stuff

start livin',
that's
the next thing
on

I would like to thank the love and light of my life, Stacey; my exceptional children, Emily, Dustin and Glendyn; my unconditionally supportive parents and inlaws, Norm and Jean Bishop and Dee and Ben Hill; my spiritual mentors, Dr. Robert Prete and Dr. Mitch Johnson; my personal coach, Jack Hoos; and my four bros. You've all inspired me and helped me learn what life is really about. Much thanks to Tim James for a great song idea and for staying in the game and to my friend Donald Seitz for his undying commitment to making this book a reality. I would like to dedicate "My List" to my grandmother, Mary Graham Bishop, who had her last laugh last year at 100.

Rand Bishop

.

I would like thank: God for the blessings. My brothers Craig and Mark, Greg Webb, Kevin Bugg and Gary Ryan for the friendship. John Florida for being my spiritual mentor and an incredible friend. Rob Hendon for believing. Rand Bishop for the melody, the talent, and the hard work. To the two people who have shaped my character and my life—I love you, Mom and Dad. To my wife, Tara, for showing me real love, real friendship, and undying support. My world is richer and more beautiful because of you, and I love you with every ounce of me. Dedicated to the memory of my uncle, Cecil Ryan; may he rest in peace.

Tim James